What Makes a Good Bed?

A Book of Haiku

Caitlyn Foster

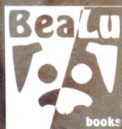

BeaLu books

BeaLu Books

ISBN Hardcover: 978-1-7341065-7-2
ISBN Paperback: 978-0-9990924-4-6

Library of Congress Control Number: 2019952458
Publisher's Cataloging-in-Publication Data is on file with the publisher.

Edited by: Luana K. Mitten
Book cover and interior design by Tara Raymo • creativelytara.com

Printed in the United States of America
October 2019

BeaLu Books
Tampa, Florida

www.BeaLuBooks.com

PHOTO CREDITS: Cover: © Mona R; Page 1: © Sonja Filitz; Page 3: © Africa Studios; Page 4: © Simon Annable; Page 5: © Ng Yin Jian; Page 6: © Sheldon Fernandez; Page 7: © Stormolino; Page 8: © Ivan Kurmyshov; Page 9: © kyslynskahal; Page 10: © Patlaya Photography; Page 11: © Andrey E. Donnikov; Page 12: © Irina Sen; Page 13: © KPegg; Page 14: © Alex Master; Page 15: © Ilike; Page 16: © Africa Studio; Page 17: © kdshutterman

What makes a good bed?

A hole in the ground,
Surrounded by taller grass
Under thick bushes

Makes a good bed for a rabbit.

Rabbits can sleep with their eyes open if they do not feel safe in their environment.

A cool shady rock,
Avoiding the heat of day,
Shallow waters near

Makes a good bed for a tiger.

A tiger's home is often called a den. They choose dens that are in quiet areas with easy access to water and prey.

ZZZ

A dark musky cave
Upside down, hanging by feet
Chilling, damp blackness

Makes a good bed for a brown bat.

ZZZ

Bats are nocturnal. They sleep during the day and are awake at night.

A tunnel below
Twists and turns in the dry dirt
Snuggled up in heaps

Makes a good bed for a meerkat.

Meerkats sleep cuddled together in heaps. The alpha meerkats, or the ones in charge, sleep in the middle of the pile to avoid any possible danger.

ZZZ

A warm, salty sea
Floating belly up in water
Entangled in kelp

Makes a good bed for an otter.

ZZZ

To avoid drifting away, otters will often sleep in kelp or seaweed. They will even link hands with other otters to create what is called an otter raft.

A cozy pillow
Near a warm, smoldering fire
Quiet, sleepy home

Makes a good bed for a house cat.

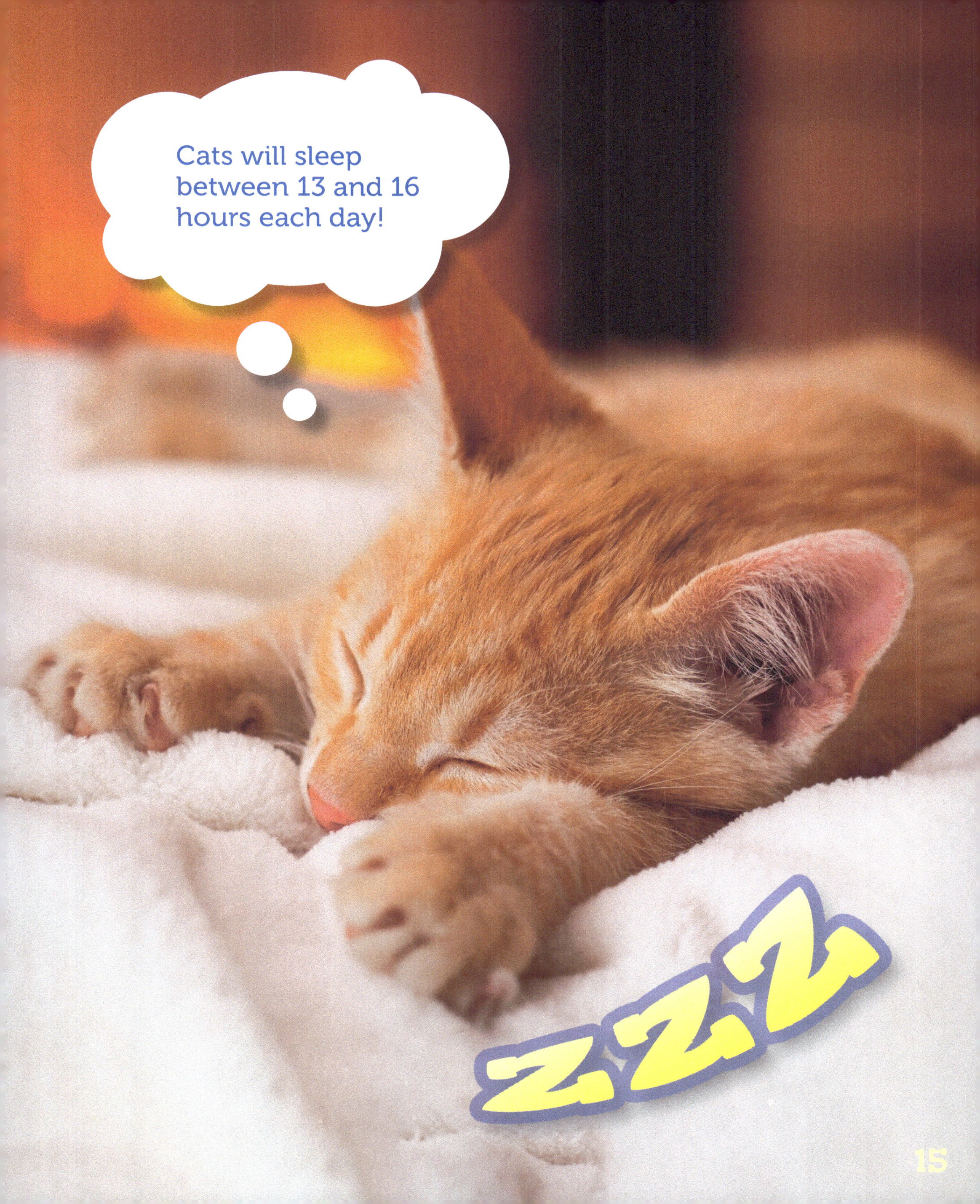
Cats will sleep between 13 and 16 hours each day!
ZZZ

A springy mattress
Beneath toasty, soft blankets
Warm, glowing night-light

Makes a good bed for you!

Shhhhh.... Everyone is sound asleep.

A book of Haiku

A haiku is a Japanese poem. Haiku are three lines long and do not rhyme. The first line contains five syllables, the second line contains seven syllables, and the third line contains five syllables.

About the author:

Caitlyn Foster was born and raised in Tampa, Florida. She graduated from the University of South Florida with her degree in Elementary Education. She is continuing education at USF and has a passion for teaching and writing.

www.ingramcontent.com/pod-product-compliance
Lightning Source LLC
Chambersburg PA
CBHW061155030426

42336CB00003B/48